MW01292097

EXPERIENCE
ANGELS

EXPERIENCE ANGELS

Melanie Beckler
www.Ask-Angels.com

Contents

Introduction

Connect with Your Angels

The angel messages found in the pages of this book, originated as audio channeled messages, that have been transcribed. If you would like to experience one of these messages as an audio meditation, and to receive updates as I release new messages in the future, simply enter your name and email into the form found here:

www.ask-angels.com/experiencing-angels-bonus-meditations

Angels are powerful spiritual beings, who are exist in a realm which is really quiet close to the physical. As humanity continues to move forward in conscious awakening, away from fear and darkness and into the light of Divine love angels are powerfully supportive allies on our path.

While angels do not exist in our physical realm, angels will often say that they are always a breath away, which simply means their realm is able to be accessed by taking a deep breath, quieting your mind, opening your heart, and focusing within.

Angels deliver messages from the Divine, to assist you in remembering your own Divine nature, the full light of your authentic self, including your Divine Light, gifts, and personal power.

It is from within the quiet, sacred stillness within, that the love, guidance and frequency of the angels can be fully known and experienced.

Angels exist as one spiritual vibration of consciousness, serving as messengers of the Divine, and yet at the same time there are different types of Angels, who specialize in a multitude of areas. The channeled angel messages in this book will assist you in connecting with the vibration of the angels. As you implement the techniques you learn, and remove layers of filters blocking your connection with the Divine and angelic realms, you will be begin to clearly and vividly experience the angels for yourself.

Right now, you have at least two guardian angels who are with you right. Your guardian angels are always looking out for you, and available to offer guidance, healing, and protection. For the most part guardian angels have never lived lives as humans or incarnated on Earth, a few have, but the majority haven't.

The specific guardian angels who are with you can change throughout your life, as you delve into new areas of growth and study, or as you move onto new lessons, but always the role of your guardian angels remains similar.

You have one guardian angel, whose purpose is to nudge

you in the right direction. They lovingly encourage you to make choices which keep you in line with your Divine blueprint, and the Divine purpose and mission of your higher self. This "nudging angel" knows and understands your spiritual gifts, talents and can see your authentic truth, highest purpose, and full potential. This angel encourages you to shine brightly always, by sending you little thoughts, inspirations and intuitive nudges which guide you forward on your path towards love and joy, while nudging you away from danger and toxic or negative situations.

You also have a guardian angel whose primary responsibility is to offer you unconditional love, comfort, and energetic support in challenging times. The voice and energy of your "comforting angel" will often come to you through the gentle and quiet voice of your intuition, or will appear as signs and signals from all around. The signs of your angels which become more and more apparent as you learn to look for them, and as you increase your conscious awareness.

Whenever you're sad, lonely, challenged, or are disappointed, remember that you have many angels around you at all times. Right now, your angels are all around you, but angels aren't experienced with our physical senses of touch, taste, sight, smell or hearing, but rather true angelic experiences occur to us through our Divine and psychic senses.

Through the channeled angel messages in this book, you will be guided and assisted in turning on, and tuning into your spiritual, and subtle senses. You will be guided to lift in consciousness to connect with the Divine, and to then tune into experience your angels.

Psychic information, including the presence and guidance of angels can be received through psychic visions, through hearing, sensing, knowing, as well as through impressions of thoughts and feelings.

While you definitely have the ability to perceive and experience angels in all of the ways above, you likely have one primary sense that you're particularly attuned to. Everyone does, and everyone is different, this is the skill that is especially strong for you. Your main psychic or subtle sense may be clairvoyance, or clear vision, but it could also be hearing, smelling, knowing, perceiving, understanding, or feeling.

You may be looking to see your angels, but if your main sense is hearing, you're likely to miss much of what is being communicated to you, at least initially.

My first psychic sense to open was feeling, and when I first started experiencing Angels I didn't see them, or hear them, but I knew their presence, and felt their incredible loving energy and frequency. When I focused in on this, my supporting senses of clairaudience (hearing), clairvoyance (seeing), and clairsentience (knowing) also began to come into focus.

The key is to just pay attention, and to be open to how you experience the Angels, and if you hear a message in your mind that may seem like you're making it up, it may seem like your imagination, but if it's loving and to the point, and if it feels good, trust that this is a true experience of angels. With trust, intention, and persistence, the love and guidance of angels will become clearer, more real, and easier to experience.

True angel experiences are comfortable, uplifting and

often exciting, they make you feel good, safe, and loved. Angels will never try to scare you, nor will they judge you or others.

If you're attempting to connect with your angels and you receive foreboding information, feel judgment, or you feel afraid, know that you may be experiencing interference from your ego, or even from an earthbound spirit, or from a being or entity who is not of the light.

Angels will help you to feel peaceful, loved, and blessed. If you're ever trying to connect with angels, and you don't feel loved, and the guidance you receive is dark, cold, or negative, stop immediately. Ask to be surrounded with Divine White Light, with 100,000 angels of love, light and protection, and then clear your mind, and begin again, because the frequency, feeling, and messages of angels, are always loving, uplifting, and inspiring!

The final two types of angels I want to mention, and then we'll get into the channeling, are the Archangels, and Nature Angels.

Archangels oversee guardian angels. They usually vibrate with an even higher frequency than the guardian angels, as they are even closer to the Divine. Archangels will help anyone who calls upon them, and they are able to do this because they operate outside of time and space, so they can be with you, and me, and everyone else who calls upon them simultaneously. The Archangels are one cohesive unit, and yet they also manifest as individual angels with specific areas of expertise.

Archangels work closely with the Ascended Masters, and are powerful allies to call upon at any time. To link with the Archangels you will need to lift your vibration. Archangels can "lower their energy down" some to connect with you, but for the most profound, clear, and powerful experience of the Archangels first elevating your energy to connect with the Divine, and then calling upon Archangels will provide the best result. (You will learn several techniques to do this in the chapters which follow.)

Nature Angels manifest as fairies, or elementals, or divas, whose main focus is to serve and assist the natural world, and the people who are called to serve in this area as well. They are the spiritual beings who are environmental helpers.

Nature Angels throughout history have often been perceived as being a bit mischievous, and this is because Nature Angels or fairies do actually have egos. They're a little bit denser than guardian angels or archangels in vibration (closely tied to the Earth Plane), but they are instantly able to tell your commitment to the environment. When you open to communicating with Nature Angels, they will often enlist you in their plan to help bring healing to the planet and the natural world. So, if you are inspired to work with the environment, calling on Nature Angels can be can be good and a positive experience, just be sure to lift your vibration first by linking directly with the Divine to skip any of the mischievous attributes of the Nature Angels, and connecting rather with their Divine qualities of love, compassion, and service, for the highest and greatest good, according to Divine Will.

In the physical realm, we all have ego's, and our ego is often the biggest obstacle to connecting with Angels. Because Angels are always around, always present, and close by, the ego mind, which chooses to focus in the physical realm has learned to filter them out. The ego is a trickster, and it muddles the mind with confusing thoughts, doubts, and fears that will actually cut you off from your psychic senses and being able to experience the angels.

Quieting the ego is the first step in experiencing angels. This is how we're going to begin now, by just taking a deep breath, and letting go of thoughts.

Take a moment to breathe, and just be. Let your mind be still and calm. With a quiet mind, and an open heart, you can meet, and experience your angels.

If there is a certain intention you would like to set, of what you want to experience as you go through this material, I invite you to set that now, just in your mind, place your intention.

Because regardless of me being able to hear you or not, the angels hear you, and they will address your intentions. So whatever you want to experience, set your intention, and then allow yourself to detach from the outcome. But remain aware, as the angels will speak to you through the words in this book, and through the quiet of your heart, and the space between words, sentences and paragraphs.

Know that whatever you experience as you read this book, is for the highest good, and that you can connect with your Angels today, and moving forward with increased clarity and frequency.

Fully experiencing angels takes commitment, it takes practice, and it takes a few techniques which are going to get into now.

First, setting the space. When I connect with the angels, I like to be in a clean, safe, and quiet place. Soft, pretty, or angelic music can also help to put you in the right calm, relaxed, present and aware state to make the connection with your angels. Then you want to cleanse the air, creating a sacred space.

I'm going to "cleanse the air now" by calling in white light, and calling in 100,000 angels to surround us, to raise our vibration, and to assist us in quieting our minds and opening our hearts, so that we may fully begin to experience the angels and the Angelic Realm.

You can also light a candle, burn some white sage, or really whatever you intuitively feel guided to do, to enter into a relaxed peaceful state, fully present in this now moment.

Thank you for this opportunity to share the experience of the angelic realm,

With love and gratitude,

Melanie

I invite you to join me now in taking a deep, relaxing breath, as you begin to focus your awareness within.

Breathe, and relax.

At this time, I ask that we be surrounded Divine White Light, and with 100 Thousand angels of healing, love, light, and protection.

I ask that each of our highest, best, most loving possible guides and angels come in, lift us in wings of love, and assist us in quieting our minds, and in opening our hearts, to tune in to the Divine love, wisdom, and guidance present at this time.

I ask that each of our guides and angels assist us in tuning into our subtle and psychic senses, which will most serve now, in paving the pathway to the Divine realms and experiencing the angels.

I now invite the highest, best, most loving possible channeling guides or angels of the light who can most serve at this time, please come in, connect, and channel through me now...

1

Journey to the Spiritual Realm

~ Archangel Metatron

Dearest one, indeed, we are here. I, Archangel Metatron, am pleased to connect with you at this time to assist you in journeying into the realm of spirit, to experience the Divine love present in this parallel dimension you are always connected to, whose door has always been open.

From where you are, you are able to attune yourself to the healing vibrations of the Divine, to the inner light and strength of your spirit, and for the purpose of perceiving, being aware, and experiencing beyond the physical, outside of your present perception and understanding.

And so at this time relax your mind, relax your eyes, your face, your neck, relax your shoulders, arms, and hands. Relax your stomach, back, and legs. Relax your feet.

Relax and breathe, and open your heart, and simultaneously Divine love is broadcast into your space, to assist you in relaxing, and lifting higher, to assist you in dropping in to the realm of Divine love and peace found within, the realm of spirit.

At this time I'm going to count backwards from 3, at which point you will be fully present in this spiritual realm.

Simply open your heart and let this occur, not analyzing how you enter into this realm, but just letting your imagination, your intuition, and your perception beyond the veil attune you to this throne of spirit.

Relax, breathe, go deeper inside, and in 3, 2, 1...

You are now present in the realm of spirit. In the Divine realm of healing, well being, and unconditional love. When you enter this space, your body naturally absorbs healing energy through this relaxed, peaceful vibration you're experiencing now.

When you enter this space, your spiritual gifts and abilities are activated and attuned through relaxing your mind and experiencing, feeling, imagining, sensing, and knowing that you are present here and now in the realm of spirit.

At this time, we invite your guardian angel to step forward and stand before you now. Relax, and notice the energetic signature, the vibration and frequency of your guardian angel.

Perhaps you've felt this before in your normal life, or this may be a new experience. Breathe, and imagine what your guardian angel looks like as they impress a visual, a feeling, even a message now upon your consciousness, to connect with you effortlessly. For you are present in the realm of spirit.

Through this connection now, the pathway is illuminated so that the guidance, healing, and wisdom of your guardian angel becomes more accessible to you at any time. The lesson in learning to connect effortlessly and frequently is to return to the realm of spirit through relaxing, breathing, opening your heart, intending, and imagining it so.

Still present with your guardian angel now, we ask on your behalf for your guardian angel to offer you a blessing or healing of Divine frequency.

Relax and breathe in this healing energy broadcast now from the angel who has been with you through your entire life, who was seen your lowest lows and highest highs and who loves you unconditionally. Your guardian angel who sees your Divine path and blueprint, the objectives your soul laid out for your lifetime, who understands the choices you have made, the opportunities you've taken or passed, and who Divinely realigns you now with love, and urges you in the direction of accomplishing your soul mission and purpose in its greatest, broadest sense of experiencing all that you are.

You guardian angel assist you in integrating all this Divine light into your body and physical life, and sharing your inner light, shining your inner light to benefit this Earth realm, to benefit humanity and all souls, and all beings across all dimensions and universes and paradigms, across the lines of time.

For you are, in this and every moment, infinitely connected to all past, present, future, alternate realities, alternate planes of experience, all united in the present moment. And so with love, with healing, and frequency, present in the spiritual realm, your guardian angel effortlessly realigns you according to Divine will, for your highest and greatest good, with joy, love, and well being.

Breathe and now receive the message of what your guardian angel most wishes to share with you at this time.

Relax, and receive the message from your guardian angel, with your spiritual and psychic senses of sensing, imagining, perceiving, feeling. Allow this guidance from your guardian angel to be impressed upon your consciousness now.

With love and gratitude, they share their light and guidance, impressing upon you the direct love of the Divine, rejuvenating your spiritual being and further activating and opening your gifts of spirit, and your natural ability to perceive beyond the physical realm, in the realm of spirit.

Experiencing not with your normal senses of touch, taste, sight, and smell, but with your spiritual, subtle, psychic senses that quietly and gently allow the guidance of the Divine, allow the experience beyond the physical, to be known, felt, and understood by you. You are translating Divine light into a way which you can understand. Know that this is a uniquely personal process. Know that your imagination, feeling, and subtle senses are your tools for perceiving in the realm of spirit, and as you connect, commune, and enjoy this connection with the spiritual realm, these subtle senses become more precise, awakened, and activated, allowing you to more clearly know and understand the guidance of your angels, guides, and, indeed, your soul.

The door to the spiritual realm is always open, but it is your choice in whether you walk through, and whether you pull back the curtains and step into experiencing beyond the veil. Your angels are always a breath away, when you relax, quiet your mind, open your heart, and enter in.

At this time we offer you a cleanse of Divine light, which pours all around you now, washing away stress, tension, and doubt, melting these denser vibrations accumulated through physical reality, and dissolving them into Divine light.

Let density go, so that the true, authentic light of your spirit can brightly shine through. Breathe, and the light that is all around you cycles throughout your physical being, releases toxins stored at a mental or cellular level into the light.

Empowering you now with this Divine light to be aware, and to choose the energy you accept and take on, to embrace the blessings of the light and of your Divine spirit.

I, Archangel Metatron, invite you now to return your awareness to your physical being, refreshed and rejuvenated, carrying with you the love, the healing of the spiritual realms and your guardian angel.

Know, that you can return at any time to connect, to rejuvenate, and to experience complete, authentic, Divine love in 3, 2, 1.

You are refreshed, awakened, and ready to share your light with all those surrounding.

I am Archangel Metatron and I am so pleased to connect. Goodbye for now.

2

Ascending the Staircase of Light

~ Archangel Uriel

Greetings beloved. Indeed, I Archangel Uriel, am present now in frequency and consciousness. I am pleased now to connect with you on multiple levels to illustrate the power you contain to create positive change and transformation in your life and in the greater whole of Planet Earth and the collective consciousness of humanity.

And so to link with my vibrational frequency now, which I am lowering down from the angelic realm, I invite you to imagine a staircase of light appearing before you.

Take this staircase one step at a time. Move up as your vibration is elevated with each step you take. Ascend in vibration now to merge with I, Archangel Uriel, and as you continue to imagine you are ascending up the staircase of light before you, I lower my vibration down to surround you with unconditional love and white light.

And so open your heart, your mind, all your chakras, and we are able to connect now.

Know that, yes, your choice, your action, your thought, and, indeed, your frequency play a vital role in the future that is unfolding.

Your consciousness merges with the collective to create the greater experience of all on Planet Earth. And so, indeed, when you see and experience challenges in your physical realm on the mass scale, when there is violence, when there is struggle, when there is manipulation as indeed, there is now at this present time, you are not hopeless.

There is help. You have the gifts of the Divine to create, to co-create in this realm, to alleviate struggle, and to infuse positivity, blessings, and frequency.

A foundation for these co-creative efforts is learning to control your mind, your spirit, and your emotions. Meditation is a valuable tool in this, your process of learning to create in the physical realm and to experience your angels.

The meditative ability to practice thought control, being able to meditate, to clear your mind, to enter into the silence, to elevate in frequency at any time, will serve you. For as I mentioned, your thoughts are creating, and so by taking control of the thoughts which spiral around in your head, you take control of the possibilities which manifest in the paradigm of your experience.

When you are focused upon something you do not really want, when you are focused on how bad things are going in your realm, when you are focused on what you are afraid of, what you dislike and fear, you are in a subconscious and subtle way focusing on manifesting these very fears and worries into your experience. Luckily a positive thought is far more powerful than the negative. This is why you are still here. This is why humanity continues forward, for negative thought far outweighs the positivity that is infused into consciousness on the collective scale for human beings at this time.

For this reason, it is of paramount importance for you to take this work you are engaged in seriously, and to have fun with it at the same time.

What I mean is to take control of your mind, to empower your life by filtering out the thoughts and fears that you don't really desire through meditation. And so when you notice you are thinking, pondering, wondering about something that is not positive, that you do not desire, that if it did manifest it would bring challenge and struggle and pain, stop. You have the choice to step back.

You are not your thought, you are the creator of the thought. And so step back and imagine that you are drawing a circle around the thought you have just placed into the manifestation queue. And since this is not something you really desire, draw a circle around it and a big black or red X through. Cancel, clear, delete, release this thought back into the light and now is the opportunity for fun. Now is the opportunity to play with your power, to claim your co creative abilities, to re-infuse your mind and your vibration with what you do desire.

A positive glimpse, a constructive idea, a seed of thought planted into your consciousness is powerful. And yest as is the case, when growing plants or food or herbs in your realm, planting is not all you must do. You must feed this seed, water it, provide light, provide hope, and, indeed, take action, for it is your thought and your vibration and your emotion and your action combined with intention and focus and persistence that ensures your success in creating blessings. Neutralize and release the negative thoughts that do enter in, releasing attachment and pain held in regard to tragedy you experience on a collective or global scale. This is not to say to de-sensitize yourself to these tragedies, but rather to play your part in shifting the field. Draw a circle around the tragedy you are experiencing, a giant X through it, and release it into the light. And then through the power of meditation, still, silent, peaceful calm, you are contributing peace by default to the collective field of manifestation.

There is great power which, indeed, has been scientifically proven in your realm that individuals coming together and meditating in a group has the power and the frequency to directly shift what manifests in the outer world. And so if you are one who is wondering why? What is wrong with the world I live in? What can I do to influence it in a positive way? I hand you now the reigns of control, the ability to create, and encourage you to meditate, to heal your own internal, mental, and emotional realm.

This is not something you do today and release and it is done for all of time. Many masters have come before and have said, "Love in every moment." Indeed love and peace in every moment will lay the foundation for a positive future."

And so your task and your objective is to remain aware and alert, for with this awareness you are able to quickly perceive and know whether or not you are thinking and vibrating and manifesting in a direction that is positive, that is helpful, and constructive, and that serves all souls in all universes on Planet Earth and in all realms, or not.

Experience Angels

With this perspective, with service, and with love, you are able to release possibilities and outcomes which are already in the process of unfolding. Through love, service, gratitude and forgiveness, density is released. And again when you find you are thinking or focusing or dwelling on something you do not want, or if a negative thought pops into your head, of something about of how bad or hard or challenging things are, draw a circle of light around this thought and an X through it signifying to the universe, to the Divine, to the angels, and to all, this is not what I'm creating. Cancel, clear, delete, release. And so it is done, and now is your opportunity to re-infuse the field with what you do want.

Now is your opportunity to plant a seed of intention that will serve all, or to simply meditate.

Enter in, quiet your mind, open your heart, activate your spiritual light, surround your energetic field with peace, love, joy, and harmony, and through this you are planting these seeds in the collective field of consciousness.

The more who meditate, who claim the co-creative reigns, who inspire peace and love and joy, the more the impact of karma individually and collectively will be lessened. The rise of light and love and joy will occur.

Taking control in this way, monitoring your thoughts, choosing to only contribute blessings of well being, joy, love, and peace to the collective field of consciousness which through consciousness and subconsciousness and super-consciousness is creating in every moment.

Claim your ability to consciously create with your conscious mind and begin paving the pathway to heal your subconscious and your super-conscious as well. On another note, there are still fragments, attachments, and forces of darkness and destruction which are present in your world.

But do not fear, remember that a positive thought far outweighs the power of a negative thought. The power of the light far outshines any darkness and negativity.

And so I offer to you now a simple protective sheath of white light all around you, first forming in an orb of white around your body, mind, and spirit. Now, with your consciousness and with your imagination, mold this light into protective armor that suits you.

You may imagine a knight's armor and a shield of white light around your body. You may imagine this light begins to cling to your energy like you are the silver surfer. You may imagine this white light as a coating on your entire body that repels negativity, that releases density, that keeps you in a high, light, and fine vibration.

Your imagination is a tool in your spiritual tool belt to create, and so use it now to imagine building with this light that is white, that we flow your way now, strengthening your protective shield.

And now another wave, another surge, another inflow of light on strands from the Divine, like beads stringing down a spider web, enter into this very moment refilling the light orb around you. This light orb which can remain intact, which will serve you in your second layer of protection, an orb of white light so that any negativity that comes in contact with you is automatically released into the light, so that density of others, fragments as you are walking down the street, attachments that may wander into your space do not effect you in vibration or in frequency.

For inside the light, inside your shield, you are able to retain peace, love, radiant well being, and joy. These emotions, these tangible elements of creation serve you always and so surround yourself with this light and love.

Be aware. Filter out negative thinking and feelings, releasing them consciously into the light and return moment to moment to love, to joy, and to peace for these serve you and serve all in transforming your realm away from duality and fear and struggle and anchoring the new paradigm of love already present in physical form, but simply needing focus, and awareness from many in order to become the standard or default mode of experience.

As you elevate your frequency and vibration, walking up the staircase of light, calling in light and angels and the Divine, your power to create with love and intention is magnified again.

The law of attraction is a piece of the puzzle but not the whole of creating in the physical. In addition to intention, your action is required. And moving forward, your link with the Divine, your link with your higher self and with your angels can only be reached through raising your vibration way up.

When you unite with your higher self, with your power, and with your spiritual light; infusing love, peace, meditative blessings, joy, and taking constructive action becomes far easier, becomes aligned.

Through connecting with your higher self, guides, and angels you will be in alignment with Divine love, which holds the power to heal, transform, and inspire.

In this moment, with light all around, imagine that we together and all who are reading these words and experiencing these frequencies and connecting with this light across the lines of time, now broadcast together a wave of ohm, a wave of peace, of love, and of gratitude broadcast out, and shared freely with all in the physical realm, the spiritual realm, the mental realm, and the emotional realm.

All realms are infused now with this wave of love, peace, understanding and joy, which is transmitted now, freely flowing, positively influencing all. Notice how good this automatically helps you to feel, for when you send light, the light returns to you multiplied.

When you share love with another, more love comes into your life. Giving in this way increases what you will receive, Serving opens the doors for so much goodness to enter into your experience, to transform your world, your life, and this moment with love, peace, and well being.

I offer you my assistance always. I will always call when answered. If you desire a more real, a more profound, a more powerful experience when connecting with I, Archangel Uriel, or when connecting with your own guides of the light and guardian angels, utilize the staircase of light. Spirit guides and angels, star beings and guardians exist in very fine vibration, we are able to lower down somewhat to merge with you in the moment, but as you elevate more of the benefit of our realm is able to be infused into your being.

And so lift yourself in vibration and in love, for these forces of the universe will serve you greatly and significantly in co-creating and in bringing peace and love and light fully into this realm.

Every moment is your opportunity. There is an infinite

supply of white light and love which you can tune into when called upon. Awareness is essential and the moment is ever now.

Cancel, clear, and release, that which does not serve and which you do not really desire, and re-infuse peace, harmony, and well being. This choice you make serves all.

Collectively your planet can be freed from the constraints of fear and manipulation and struggle one being, one spark of the Divine, one meditative now moment at a time.

Choose peace, choose love, choose well being, release your fear and doubt, cancel it out, and re-inspire this realm, for you have that ability. Your ascension, your upliftment in frequency will subtly and directly influence all humans. In mass, this is extraordinarily powerful to meditate, to intend, to plant seeds, and to create together a positive future, a new pathway, an inspiring future centered and grounded in Divine love.

I, Archangel Uriel, leave for now as I broadcast another surge of light your way. Open and lift. Breathe and feel this infinite, Divine love which you can now carry with you into your day, which you can reunite with in any moment with awareness, with focus, and with practice. You can pave your pathway to the future with positivity, peace, and love. Again, this serves you, yes, but the blessings, the ripple far and wide extending out, serving all souls in all universes through love.

I leave you now with my blessing, with white light, with unconditional love, and so it is. For now, I am complete. Goodbye for now.

3

Uniting With The Divine

~ Archangel Metatron

Greetings dearest one, indeed I Archangel Metatron am here. I greet you in this present moment and say to you, indeed, your inner world and state of being mirrors your outer world. And the outer world around you, mirrors your inner state of being.

These separate worlds, without and within, are linked so that you can impact your inner environment by taking action in creating change in your outside world. This much is true. You can feng shui your home, de-clutter your space, open windows to let sunshine light in, light candles, or burn sage. Yes, these are things which will cleanse out your outer reality, and when you do this, there are less distractions and you will find it easier to quiet your mind and enter in. You will find it easier to connect with the truth and the light and the love of your heart, and the guidance of your angels found within you.

But know that energy flows the other way as well, and so you can burn all the sage you like, practice feng shui, and de-clutter your home, your office, and your outer world, but if your inner realm is cluttered with thought, with doubt, with worry, and with beliefs that do not serve you, you will still feel challenged, blocked, and overwhelmed. Clutter from within, so without.

And so as you would de-clutter or clean your home, which is of course recommended, we angels in the realms above, encourage you and say to you, now is a powerful time to clean your inner being as well.

Meditate, and join your angels in this meditation space now, clear your mind, and enter in. Feel, within your inner world, the still, peace, and calm. You may not find this peaceful serene bliss right away, it may not be there right away. You may attempt to enter in, and immediately begin to think of 10 things you should be doing, or 10 people who you have something to say to.

But for right now, let these things go.

Release all thought into the light of the Divine which is all around you, and enter into your heart. Enter into love, enter into the sacred space found within.

Enter into the the still, silent, inner calm. Imagine you are opening your heart, feel your energy pull inward, and now unite with your spirit, with the inner light, your inner flame, which brightly shines within you.

By quieting your mind, and entering in you can learn to hear the authentic voice of your soul, and the guidance of your angels. However, to clearly hear this wisdom, and guidance, and encouragement, there is a filtration process, a cleaning process, and a process of letting go of the doubts that appear. Letting go of the trickster, or "naysayer" that is your ego mind. Letting go of worrying, of wondering, of thinking of a million things at once, which leads to a downward spiral of thought that carries you away. Let go of this.

Clear your inner space, by focusing on the light that you found within, and all around, and as you dive into this light with your conscious awareness it expands.

Yes, we angels broadcast strands of light your way to assist you in increasing your vibration now. To assist you in clearing your mind, and filling your inner realm with pure love, light, and well-being from the Divine.

Clear mind. Open heart. Activated spiritual light. This is your triple threat, this is your trio to heal your inner realm, and to experience your angels.

Understand that when you enter into your heart, surrendering to the still and calm and peace of the moment, you are able to link directly with the Divine, with Divine love, and with the Divine purpose, plan, and paradigm for your life.

Entering in, opening your heart, breathing, and just being. There is magic in this process. From within this inner silence, you connect with the angelic realms, and from therein all planes of existence are available to you.

You are able to connect with them, though to do so, in a safe and rewarding manner, we offer you this process.

Breathe, and let your mind be still and calm. As thoughts do emerge and appear, imagine that you are releasing them into the light, changing their course, so that they release and let go.

Open your heart, and feel your energy ground into the Earth, where you are able to feel your oneness with Earth, with the light, and with All That Is.

Let this beautiful, healing light you find at the core of the Earth flow throughout your being, around you, within you, and now let it flow up. Up through the Earth, up through the bottom of your feet, let it flow up, let each of the chakras of your physical body be balanced, be purified, and be activated to their highest possible extent, the rotation and frequency of each aligned for your benefit.

Continue to lift up with the light, now up above your crown, and above the lights. Go up, with consciousness, and seek direct connection with the Divine, with God, with Divine Love, and with Spirit

Lift and go up. Know that this is your birthright to make this connection, and with your intention to connect you are able to do so now.

Go up, and unite with the Divine. Now, feel your Oneness with this Divine light you find, and notice that you are not separate, but One.

Open your heart, and let the love and the light of the Divine flow throughout your entire being.

Let yourself be lifted and illuminated by this Divine light. A new level and degree of Divine light will be downloaded into your awareness now. Assisting you in making this connection with the Divine now and with your Angels in the future.

And now receiving the full benefit of your connection with the Divine light in this now, open your heart. Let the light of the Divine infiltrate the silence of your mind, healing any aspects or attributes of your mind that are still in density and are ready to be illuminated.

Breathe... Relax...

Understand that simply being in this place of direct presence with the Divine is a noteworthy experience. Honor the Divine, thinking; "Thank you, help me, assist me, heal me." For indeed all of these manifestations are available to you.

Simply connecting with Divine light offers you a healing, but the most powerful is when you connect, and when you realize that you are one with the Divine and with All That Is. Feel this. Experience this.

Unite with the healing made available through this, and now ground the light of the Divine into your life, by once more feeling your awareness ground.

Imagine roots, or a column of light flowing down from the bottom for your feet, anchoring you to the Earth and through this anchoring, all the light particles, Divine strands of love are anchored with you as well.

Grounding the light from the Divine into physical form where it becomes available for all.

Ground light from the Divine into physical form to bring these blessings of the Divine into your own life, and to benefit all.

Feel that your energy has now been cleansed. Your inner state of being cleansed and realigned, along with the energy of your aura, your mind, and your body.

Let your vibration lift and open, and still in the presence of Divine love, you may ask:

"Where in my inner realm, my inner world, my thoughts, beliefs or, subconscious are there patterns or paradigms stored that do not serve me in manifesting blessings in the outside world."

Enter in. Open. Notice. And let this go.

"Angels, please take this limiting belief and release this belief into the light", and ask that it be replaced with a feeling of knowing, of being loved by the Divine. Witness this release and be replaced with Divine love.

Now, on your own, what in you is blocking you from truly manifesting blessings in your outside world? From within, so without.

Open your heart. Quiet your mind. Tune into in what you need to release. Be aware, and now let it go. Release into the light, and over to the Angels. Witness this release as the particles of whatever is needing to go arc actually pulled out of your being, like a gray dust which dissipates into the light, and in the space in which these were contained, they are now replaced with what does serve you. Replaced with unconditional love, with compassion, with hope, and with light. Let this in to fill the void and as light flows in, what else is pushed out?

What else in you is ready to go? What belief, what mode of thinking, what habit, what pattern? Are you quick to anger and slow to love? Let anger rise to the surface and be healed and transformed and released into the light now. Let love in to take it's place. Let compassion in. Let joy fill the void.

As this new level of light comes in, what else is pushed out from deep within your core? What no longer serves you when you walk in the path of aligning with your full authentic light and spirit?

A thought, a belief, a pattern, a habit, a memory, a painful experience, a current challenge? Let this rise to the surface and the angels connect it with a strand of light to either lift the vibration of the characteristic transforming it completely, or releasing it 100% from your vessel. Releasing it into the light, and if this occurs you must replace it with something.

Consciously open up to invite in love, well being, joy, light, and compassion of the Divine, for the highest and greatest good.

As you let more light in, is there a block? Is there doubt? Is there worry? Let these go. And let in more light. And then what comes up? "Is this really working?" Are you doubting? Are you wondering? Release doubt. Open your heart and lift for you are in the presence of great beings of the Inner Realm.

Light of the highest possible kind is all around you now, assisting you in both clearing your outer world and recharging the vibration, bringing love, joy, hope, compassion, and excitement all around you. And letting yourself fill up from within as well, with love, with peace, with still, silent, calm, competence.

From within, and from without, you have received Divine light and healing now.

Open your heart. Breathe. And know that you are now able to share these blessings with the world around you. Grounding your light into the physical is the first step, and then, love is the second. For when you respond with love, when you love, you continue the healing in your own life and you create a ripple of love throughout existence that benefits all.

Love is powerful beyond measure.

The ripple effect from one loving action is significant, and so begin with you, with loving yourself, with nurturing yourself with taking excellent care, with honoring your inner light in divinity through healthy food, through dance, through celebration. This activates you more.

Your joy, your love, your hope, these positive vibrations actually metaphysically carry you forward along on your path of awakening. Bringing you into alignment with the experience that you sought out to have here in the physical. Bringing you into alignment with experiencing your angels.

Doubt, fear, and anger, lead you astray. Do not worry when they come up, feel, release, and let whatever dense emotion came up, go.

Let it go. That's why it came up, and let it be replaced with light, with hope, with love and with compassion.

These forces of the Universe will usher you forward.

Prioritize and practice connecting directly with the Divine through your self, for through this connection there are many benefits for you and for all you encounter.

Open to experience this connection. Love willingly. Love freely. Love fully. This is your path to full awakening and yes, take time to clear your mind, to heal from within. Your growth and healing brings many blessings in the world around you and outside of your personal experience. In all ways, love serves. Love inspires. Love is the master path to awakening your full potential, and so get started, and get going.

Connect with the Divine. Connect through opening your heart, and lifting. Opening your mind and embracing the light of the Divine, and now ground all of this light, flowing it down into the physical.

Feel roots flowing down. Feel a column of light flowing down from the Divine into your body and continuing down grounding into the Earth, below the ground, below the roots, and into the core of light at the center of the Earth.

Grounding light from the Divine for the highest and greatest good for your benefit and for the benefit of all.

And now the turn to awareness, your physical being, return to the room, notice that within you, and outside of you, you have received a light infusion. Filling your space without and within, with love, with joy, and compassion. So that you may ride the wave of light present upon the planet. Creating a ripple effect of the highest order and form through walking your master path and Divine blueprint, living love. living joy, and accomplishing your highest purpose here in the physical.

Shine your full light, I Archangel Metatron leave you with my blessing and say to you "Dearest one, you are loved. You are blessed and I now leave you with my blessing and with the knowing that I am on hand to assist you in linking with the Divine in this way, so that you may then increase your awareness, reduce your filters which are present, and experience your angels. Goodbye for now."

4

Pathway to the Angelic Realm

~ Archangel Uriel

Greetings dearest one. Indeed, I am Archangel Uriel present here and now to assist you in opening, clearing and lifting your frequency, and removing the filters which prevent you from fully seeing and knowing and experiencing in the realm of the spiritual.

Through opening your chakras, the spiritual centers within your physical body, and opening your mind's eye, you are able to clearly connect, experience, and know the Divine love and frequency of the angelic realm.

Indeed, your angels are always near, and present in your life according to Divine will. Angels exist in a lightened vibration outside of physical form. You are able to connect with the angelic realm through intention, focus, and by cleansing and purifying your energy. By activating your spiritual vibration, and increasing your frequency, you will be able to experience the realm of the angels. When you lift in consciousness awareness to experience this high vibration-al place, we are then able to connect, commune, serve and assist you in continuing to progress forward.

In this book you will learn practical techniques. You will be guided through your personal experience to transcend physical reality. So get ready to set aside your mind and enter into the realms of spirit through your heart, your chakras, and your spiritual light.

Indeed angels are able to connect with you directly in the physical realm. This however is far outside of our normal experience of pure connection to source and to Divine love, and so we must lower our vibration down to make the connection with you. When you take the time to pre-pare yourself for this connection first, you are able to in-crease your clarity of experience. When you consciously lift in the light, clear and open your chakras, go up and seek God, and from the place of direct connection with source then connect with your angels, truly magnificent learning, growth, and experience of the angelic realm is made possible.

And so we will begin now with an energetic cleanse and ac-tivation. Then in the chapters to follow you will be guided to directly connect with your guardian angel and your spirit guide of the light. You will then be guided to lift even higher, to leave behind your ego mind, your physical body and way of experiencing your world, releasing these filters which focus your consciousness in the physical plane.

You will be guided to lift up and out of physical experience to unite fully and directly with the angelic realm, with the archangels, and with the full vibration, love, and magnifi-cence of your angelic, spiritual. Your higher self, the part of you that is still present in the realm of spirit, that has not gone through the forgetting process to enter into the physical. The part of you that exists still, in direct union and connection with the archangels, with the Divine, and with source.

In making this link with your higher self and angels, you're ascending, and lifting in frequency which will serve you in many ways. The ongoing teaching, guidance, and learning you will connect with is of paramount importance. The increased frequency, Divine love and vitality that you align with through connecting to the angelic realm will stay with you always. This light will illuminate your life, and will bring love's blessings to you. As you connect with and radiate love you create a ripple of positive energy, into the physical realm which you are a part of, and which you are co-creating at this time.

And so to begin the energetic cleanse of light; sit up straight, relax, place your tongue gently upon the roof of your mouth and focus on your breath. Now as you read these words, notice an orb of white light that begins to gently flow down around you. This orb of white light cleanses and illuminates your spiritual self, your talents, and gifts by releasing blockages of mind, body, soul, and spirit.

Now imagine or visualize that as this orb of light, brilliant luminescent light, flows around you, your conscious awareness begins to lift up. This orb of light from the Divine, this frequency from I Archangel Uriel, from all the archangels, from your guardians and guides, lowers down around you anchoring our presence and light into the physical and now lifts you up, out the top of this orb of light, bringing this light with you, floating up, and lifting up in consciousness.

And as you lift up out the top of this orb, the next level of cleansing takes place. For density and negativity, pain, blockages, and illness do not lift with you, but rather stay in the lower vibrations and you conscious being, aware and present, lift up into the higher light of Divine love.

We shine another spotlight down upon you now and say to you, fully activating your chakras is essential, in fully linking with first your guardian angel, who is closely connected to the physical realm. And then as you continue to lift, as you merge with your guardian angel and increase your vibration ever more, as you practice lifting up into the light, visualizing your frequency increasing, ascending the staircase of light, opening to the Divine love and light that is all around, higher levels of experience are able to be perceived and witnessed.

The archangels and the realm of your higher self exists even higher, a vibration above that of your spirit guide and guardian angel. By opening your chakras, your spiritual centers, you are enabled to lift higher, to make this link with clarity and with precision. You are able to tune into the wisdom and truth and knowledge of the archangelic and angelic realm. We are pleased and blessed to share with you, for our service in connecting you with the realms of Divine love, serves all. This is of course our intention, to love, and to serve.

Again now, a new orb of light, a strand of Divine light, shines upon you. This orb of light lowers down upon you already present in an increased place of vibration and frequency. Let this light orb lower down, opening all your chakras, opening root, sacral, solar plexus, heart, throat, third eye, crown, soul star chakra, and your upper energy centers, 12, all activating now.

Breathe as all seven of your physical bodies energy centers are activated and united, now merging in a pillar of white light which is centered along your spinal column.

This pillar of light begins to gather more love, white light, and Divine frequency from all around. Relax as the pillar of light naturally expands to encompass all your chakras and to elevate you in energy and frequency even more.

Breathe as this light continues to expands around you; protecting your mind, body, and spirit, amplifying your frequency and lifting you up in the light.

Imagine that you are lifting, floating up in consciousness as you read these words. Now consciously open your heart, breathe, and focus within.

To begin the process of experiencing your angels, we invite in your guardian angel now. Beloved being of light and love enter in. Wrap this beloved being in your wings of light to uplift them even more and help to make this link now.

Open your heart to feel, see with your mind's eye, experience through the lens of your heart, know and understand, the presence of your guardian angel with you now.

I do wish to clarify now that yes, you are connecting. Your guardian angel is present here and now. If you are not yet experiencing this in the magnitude that you would like, understand that filters are still present in your consciousness. Filters which serve you to understand the physical and spiritual realms, filters which are largely focused upon filtering out the spiritual realms and focusing you, a conscious spiritual being in the physical world, in your physical, human body.

But really, you are much more than simply a physical being, and as you merge with your guardian angel, as you practice, as you intend, and as you lift your filters will be reduced. With consistency, with persistence, with practice, and with intention to connect you will experience your angels. Opening your heart, opening your mind's eye, seeing with your clairvoyant sight, hearing through your clairaudient ears, experience your guardian angel who is indeed present now.

Your guardian angel assists in this linking process, lifting you up even more. Open your heart, breathe, and surrender to the process. Know that the love, peace, and joy you are connecting with now is the vibration of your guardian angel who is always near, and who loves you dearly.

I, Archangel Uriel now ask on your behalf, beloved guardian angel, what message or healing or comfort do you have for this beloved being now?

What can you share and help them to know and understand that will most serve?

And now you, dearest one, open your heart, quiet your mind, and tune into the feeling. Let the knowing of the message your guardian angel transmits, be made known to you now.

If you are waiting and wanting this message to audibly appear, know that you will have had to release many filters of experiencing reality prior to this taking place.

Initially it is far more likely that your guardian angel will speak to you telepathically. And so listen with your heart for the message of your guardian angel to appear. And if you receive a message of love and encouragement, an uplifting feeling, a feeling of hope, beauty, or if you feel your frequency increase, you are doing this correctly. You are tuning in to the guidance of your guardian angel.

From here, you may ask for additional guidance, ask for assistance with something you are specifically working on manifesting or healing, or you may simply choose to thank your guardian angel for showing up and, for merging with you.

To connect your guardian angel lowers their vibration down, you raise your frequency, and in this the connection is made possible. Practice sustaining high levels of love and vibration, and the clarity by which you experience your guardian angel is automatically increased.

Awareness in your physical life comes through being present in the moment. Question your belief systems, and question what you are experiencing for this will also serve you in increasing awareness, and increasing the clarity of connection with your guardian angel. Awareness serves in this way because it allows you to transcend the filters of your mind, which are largely focused on helping you to experience this life in the physical.

In any moment, there are a number of spiritual beings around you. There are spiritual frequencies, and dimensions interweaving, overlapping with your physical realm, but your mind chooses to filter much of this out. Your mind chooses to present you with the experience of being a physical human being.

But with your desire to connect with the angelic realm, you can begin to transform these filters. Right now as we shine a final orb of light upon you for this first session, we do so with the intent to release the first layer of filtration. To release your filters, which up until now, have been subconsciously filtering out the full experience of your guardian angel including their guidance, love, and wisdom. By choosing to consciously relax now you are able to release a level of filtration into the light.

Now open your heart to experience your guardian angel to a new level and a new degree. This may come in the form of feeling, knowing, seeing, hearing, a telepathic message you receive, something you become aware of, or a concept that just comes into your awareness. Your guardian angel serves and loves you and offers you now whatever it is that will most help you as you embark upon this new journey of lifting in vibration, of letting down your filters, and of vividly, really, connecting with the angelic realm.

Thank your guardian angel who is always near, and allow yourself to now return your awareness to your physical body, as our first session is almost complete.

In preparation for the next, in which we will assist you in lifting even higher, connecting more profoundly, more vividly, and directly, be aware, be present, and believe the nudgings of your heart. Quiet your mind and listen for the inner voice of your soul.

Listen for the quiet, subtle guidance from the Divine, from the universe, your heart, your guardian angel, and be aware.

Question the world around you and why things are the way they are. What is really true and valid? This awareness will assist you in releasing more filters, and will prepare you for your next experience of uniting with the angelic realm.

For now, open your heart, and consciously return your awareness to your body, and ground your now cleansed, uplifted and immensely loved spiritual self back into physical form.

Understand that all the blessings of love, light, compassion, and wisdom you connect with through this meditative state, through reaching up and uniting with the angelic realm, stays with you. Bringing long lasting healing and blessings of well being, vitality, and love into your life.

Our first lesson is now complete. I am Archangel Uriel and you are immensely loved. Continue forward, and the full experience of the angelic realm can be made known to you.

You are already connecting, now it is simply a matter of increasing your awareness, releasing your filters, and fully opening your system of spiritual receptivity, so that you may directly see, hear, know, feel, understand, and experience the angelic realm.

We will meet again soon. Goodbye for now.

5

Lifting Higher

~ Archangel Metatron

Dearest one, indeed, I, Archangel Metatron, greet you in this moment with love and with frequency. Know that you are greeted with many angels, guides of the light, and guardians of the physical realm as you enter into this space now, by becoming present and aware.

By quieting your mind and focusing on your breath, breathing, relaxing, and now feeling your energy ground, feel yourself connecting with Earth, and thereby with All That Is.

And now let all this light flow up, opening all the chakras of your physical body, uniting them in one white light, and then continuing up in consciousness above the universe, above the lights, up, and up. Feel your vibration lift and rise. You are being assisted by your guardian angel and by I, Archangel Metatron, in lifting your vibration now into a place of direct connection with source, with God, with the

One Source Energy flowing throughout All That Is, that you are a part of.

Feel, know, and experience your oneness herein, and now from this place, from an elevated vibration, in connection with the Divine... "We now invite your guardian angel, your spirit guide of the light, and your guide of the light, or angel, which serves you now in accomplishing your life purpose. Come in, connect, and assist this beloved being in lifting even more."

Know that as your chakras are fully opened, engaged with the light, they are filtering the pure, vibrant light of the Divine and translating these light codes into a manner by which they can be understood, and experienced, and comprehended in this present space and time.

As you consciously open and lift, we now place a powerful tool, an orb of white light from the Divine, all around you. At this time, this orb is likened to a magical elevator, that as you relax, breathe, and enter in, you are able to consciously teleport to another time and space. To a sacred sanctuary of spirit and of the Divine.

Imagine that you are being relocated to this sacred space now, and the beautiful blessing and benefit of this space, is that it is uniquely yours and that you can create it. And so with your imagination, with visualization, paint the picture of this Divine and sacred space of yours.

Now, are you in nature? A pristine church, or sanctuary? Are you quite simply in a realm of light? Paint this picture, this sacred place of connection with the Divine.

Now imagine that you are noticing, or finding a special box of light. This box serves to contain your mind, which may have the propensity to doubt, to question, and to keep you contained in 3D reality through the filters of your mind, which by default filter out the spiritual realms.

These filters do not serve you in clearly experiencing, seeing, feeling, and knowing in the etheric and spiritual realms, in meeting your angels and connecting with their wisdom, guidance, and love. And so imagine that you are placing your ego mind with all its filters, flaws, and strengths into this box of light. Your ego serves a purpose, yes, but for right now let yourself place your ego mind in this box of light, placing it upon the shelf in this, your sacred sanctuary, where you will return, to pick up your mind and your thoughts later. But for right now, trust and know that you are supported in putting them aside, in letting them go so that you can perceive this space not through the filters of your mind, but through the energetic centers, your chakras, which, when open and intact, can accurately and precisely translate the light of the Divine into a way you can understand, experience, and benefit from.

Notice and image that you are still present in this inner sanctuary, your sacred space, in this beautiful, illuminated place of light, fine, vibration in which many of your guides and angels have already entered in. Indeed, ascended masters from the inner realms are focusing upon this place and point in time now, pleased and happy to assist you in connecting and experiencing fully, with all of your being, the healing love, guidance, truth, and wisdom of the benevolent, loving, etheric beings that are your guides and angels, who are present here now.

Now from this place, imagine an orb, a spotlight of white light that is above your crown chakra, and another orb of white light that is below your feet. Quickly now these two orbs move down and up clearing and activating each of your body's chakras, your receptors, and translators of spiritual frequency.

Relax, open, and tune into these subtle senses of feeling, sensing, knowing, imagining, seeing with your mind's eye, hearing with your clairaudient ears, experiencing Divine love outside of physical form.

This is an important lesson and facet to note on your path of uniting with your angels, for you may expect your angels to connect with you physically through your senses, to appear miraculous before you in physical form. While this is not impossible, it is rare and you far increase your likelihood of connecting with your angels when you ascend and lift into the angelic realm.

This sacred place where you are present now, is a meeting zone so to speak, a place in between realms, not fully present in the angelic realm, and not fully present in the physical. It is a medicine wheel, a healing place of light, an alternate dimension that you can enter into through your meditation and your conscious intention, and here your guardian angel comes in.

Imagine that your guardian angel is now standing before you, radiating love and light, unconditional love and frequency of the Divine. Notice that as you open your heart, your Divine message center, you are able to understand the meaning which your guardian angel broadcasts your way now.

You are able to feel their presence, love, and tranquility. You may begin to feel a bit light headed, or enlightened, for your vibration is being increased even more. You're going higher, lifting up.

An orb of white light is all around you still, protecting you, offering cleansing and healing energetically. Working to bring you into alignment with your angels, and working to now release a level of filtration which has been blocking the spiritual realm from your experience.

Filters are created through fear, through beliefs, and through the course of your normal life in the physical. There's nothing wrong with having filters. You are a physical being and without these it would be much harder for you to retain focus in the physical realm. But the blessing you are presented with now, is the ability to choose to let down your guard, and to release the filters blocking out the realms of spirit.

Now focusing upon your mind's eye, your pineal gland in the center of your head, we send a surge of light, an activation, an orb of white light to fill this energy center.

Now with a burst of frequency, an explosion of light, your third eye is cleansed, opened and invigorated so that you may clearly see in the realm of the Divine. So that you may clearly see in the realm of the angels, to see Divine love.

Your guardian angel now wraps you in wings of love and uplifts you in vibration even more, as we now call upon your spirit guide of the light who can most serve you now, to come in.

You are lifting in vibration, and your spirit guide is lowering down. You are meeting in this sacred sanctuary, sacred place, this realm of light and love where you are safe, where you are in an increased vibration, and where these benevolent, beloved spiritual beings are able to effortlessly enter into without lowering too much, still retaining the light and magnificence of their Divine connection.

Connecting with your spirit guide now helps you to jump up to the next level in vibration, to go even higher. As you increase vibration, as you increase the light you are able to hold, you make yourself available to experience the Divine love of many high vibrational beings, for without raising your vibration, you are still able to call upon and experience the love and guidance of the ascended masters, of your higher self, and of archangels, but in a filtered down, a somewhat watered down form.

When high vibrational beings connect with you in the physical realm, they must leave a significant amount of light, and of vibration in the realms of spirit. When you meet in the middle, when you put in the work to ascend your vibration, the benefit is that these high vibrational frequencies are able to be tuned into. And when you connect with new heights, with new guides of the light, with immense levels of evolvement and of light, the frequency indeed, rubs off upon you.

When you connect in this way, lifting your vibration again to this point and beyond, it becomes easier. You pave the pathway, pave the foundation, and once you connect with your angel, your guardian angel, and your spirit guide, the path is paved even more.

Once you have lifted to make the connection, the guidance, the wisdom and the teaching can be accessed by you from a conscious place, of being fully present and aware in your normal life, in the physical realm, in the third through fifth dimensions which you are experiencing at this powerful time of life as a physical being.

Still present and aware in your sacred inner place, imagine that a circle of angels, of light, guides of light and love,

Experience Angels

ascended masters from the inner realms, form a healing circle all around you.

Each master, each being, each guide, radiates a different quality of spirituality, of highly evolved being. Broadcasting attributes such as compassion, unconditional love, joy, protection, vitality, well being, healing, and transformation. Each guide, each being, each master in this circle of light, from their heart to yours now broadcasts this unique quality your way. As you consciously open the doors of your heart, see this heart chakra center vibrating with a beautiful emerald green. This green orb of light that is your message center is becoming alive, activated, and healed as these masters of the etheric and inner realms, as angels, as guides, as the archangels share this frequency and healing with you now.

Open your heart and feel, see, know, hear, and experience in whatever psychic sense is most highlighted for you at this time, in this life. Experience this Divine healing now. Healing of your heart chakra, your spiritual body, your light body, and your entire being.

You may begin to feel very light, tingly, or you may feel nothing at all. The lesson is that the more your energy centers open, the more vividly and clearly you will experience the angelic realms.

When you call upon angels, we answer always. But you may not know, you may not experience us at all if you are engaged with your ego mind, or if your chakra energy centers are closed or blocked off. In this way you have control over how quickly you progress and open to vividly and fully experience the angelic realm.

Increasing your vibration, lifting in light and love is the

direct path, the direct route to increased clarity of connection.

Healing your heart, which now the light broadcast your way is focused in, to heal your heart chakra, this message center, to release past wounds, hurts, and blockages preventing you from fully tuning into the spiritual realms. These blocks are whisked up into the light and released, and replaced now with a surge of love. Replaced now with the full presence and light of your guardian angel who, if it is your intention, will connect with you fully now.

If it is your intention to make this link, to pave this pathway, to directly connect with your guardian angel of light and love, think or say, "I now invite my guardian angel of the light. Please come in and connect with me now."

This very link is profound and offers you healing on many different levels. You see, in working with your guardian angel in this way, you are able to increase your vibration tenfold. When you are able to vividly and clearly connect with your guardian angel, you will then know that you are ready to begin to ascend even higher, and your guardian angel will help you work with visualizations such as walking up the staircase of light, or you may choose to take an orb of light as an elevator up even higher into the realms of spirit.

You may choose to open the doors of your heart and immediately imagine that you are floating up in vibration into the realms of spirit, a process of going higher. A process you can use over and over to connect with your guardian angel, and later on with archangels directly, once your frequency has reached an elevated point and you are ready to connect, is this.

Simply center, feel your energy ground, and connect to

Earth. Feel your oneness with the Earth and understand that this oneness is not only with Earth but with all of creation, with God, with the archangels, with your higher self, with the Divine realms, with your guardian angel, with All That Is.

Feel this oneness for it opens a door for you to connect. Feel this oneness with all, for it heals and nurtures your spiritual being. Feel your oneness with All That Is. Feel the incredible warmth, and glow of this light and connection, and now let this light from the core of the Earth flow up. Let it first bring healing to your root chakra. And in between your tailbone and your belly button, your sacral chakra now receives healing, blessing, upliftment from the Divine.

This light continues to flow up clearing and activating your solar plexus and continuing up, opening your heart to a new level and degree. Now, let your throat open to clearly communicate Divine love, let your third eye become initiated and opened to clearly see in the realms of spirit, and now your crown open wide to allow Divine light enter into your being.

Now working with the first of your upper chakras, your soul star chakra, which is the first chakra completely out of your physical vibration, completely in the realm of spirit, which filters the first level of the Divine into the physical. And so your soul star chakra now receives the cleanse, a light white, orb is placed over this energetic center now and in 3, 2, 1 it bursts open with a powerful activation healing the center, releasing those filters which have blocked you from experiencing the realms of the angels and of spirit. Let them go, for they do not serve.

Let love in and simply remain focused upon your breath, upon opening your heart, upon relaxing and experiencing the love, for this is the place which you are able to receive direct guidance from the angelic realm.

Still present now in the sacred sanctuary, your magical, personal sacred space, we call upon your spirit guide of the light to enter in and to stand before you. And we ask on your behalf:

"Beloved spirit guide, what information, what message do you have for this beloved? Now, please directly communicate to their heart, mind, and spirit."

Relax, open, receive.

Receive the blessing of frequency, of healing, and of love. And now notice present in this your sacred sanctuary, with your guide, and with your guardian angel, that a doorway appears, a doorway into the higher realms, a doorway which will help you to lift up even higher in vibration and in frequency. For it is even higher that the archangels dwell and that your higher self, the spiritual part of you, fully connected to the Divine, to love, to all your power and gifts, and light, exists.

The realm of archangels is even higher than the vibration of this sanctuary, even higher than you have reached before. Imagine that you are stepping through this doorway now, and that it is actually a sort of elevator that now lifts you up.

Open your heart as you lift, and breathe in.

Exhale, to leave any density you have accumulated over the course of your life behind. And breathe in, as this elevator of light rises, lifting you up now into direct presence with Source, with the Divine, with God, with All That Is. And in this place, through a direct connection with the Divine, this is where you are able to access the archangelic realm. This is where you are able to access the truth of your higher self.

We bring you to these realms now to give you a taste of the infinite love and magnificence and your light. Simply being here soothes and heals your soul, releases blockages, and brings you into alignment with Divine love.

Now from this place, you are able to request that your higher self and that the archangels come in and connect. Know that we are already here. Witness, experience, feel the love and blessing of the archangels, of your higher self, of these spiritual etheric beings of light that exist in direct presence and communion with the Divine always.

There's so much benefit in your being here, and yet you must work your way up, to staying in this space. Must work your way up in holding the amount of frequency required to directly commune with the archangels, and to directly channel your higher self. For right now being present in this place is enough.

"We ask on your behalf, for the archangels and your higher self, to offer you a gift, a sign, a blessing that you really are in their presence."

Open your heart, quiet your mind, feel, experience with your subtle senses, receive this sign and blessing from the archangelic realm, and from your higher self.

Now, stepping back a level into your sacred sanctuary, imagine that a waterfall of light flows down all around you, soothing, cleansing, and uplifting you, bringing whatever healing you most need now.

You may now go over to the box in which your mind is safely kept. Your mind indeed, serves in many ways. And so you can gather and embrace your mind now, knowing that mind too has received a cleanse and an alignment in this space.

Collect your thoughts, and now begin to feel your energy ground, as you are returned to the physical realm. But know, that all the magnificent frequency and light you have connected with is not lost, it is with you.

You are able to share love and blessings, which serves all and which assists you in increasing your vibration even more, increasing the amount of light you are able to hold, at all times. To be a spiritual master in physical form means to retain a very high, uplifted vibration at all times. With this, you are able to link with your guardian angel, your spirit guides, and archangels at a moment's notice, with the blink of an eye, or snap of a finger.

With intention, you are able to connect. Love, of course, serves this mission. Life holds many lessons in the physical and spiritual. Your angels are pleased to guide you through this process. As you practice connection, the clarity by which you are receiving guidance will increase. And so regardless of where you are right now, regardless of what you did or did not experience in our session together today, you are able to make this link.

You are able to clearly comprehend and communicate with angels, with an open mind, an open heart, activated chakras, and a fine, high, light vibration. These are your tools. Practice, and remember the angelic realm, the ascended masters, your spirit guides are always near and always happy to connect as you increase your vibration and meet in the middle, your experience will feel much more real. The guidance you receive will increase in clarity.

Enjoy your increased vibration and practice maintaining the aura of love and joy and gratitude, knowing that the pathway between you and the angelic realm has been laid.

In the next portion of this course, you will illuminate this pathway even more to make connecting with your guardian angel and with your higher self, direct, and effortless.

I am Archangel Metatron. I am so pleased to assist. You are dearly loved and blessed and lifted. Goodbye for now. I am complete.

6

Experiencing Angels and Archangels

~ Archangel Michael

Welcome. Indeed, I am Archangel Michael. So pleased to connect with you now.

Indeed, I am the Archangel most accessible from the physical realm for my purpose is closely intertwined with serving humanity and Earth. Through the rays of the sun's light my frequency is broadcast and so at any time you may call upon me and understand I will indeed answer and connect.

I am pleased to offer protection, increased frequency, and assistance in elevating your vibration so that you might fully enter into the angelic realm to experience the wisdom and love. To assist you in increasing your vibration even more so that you may directly link with these Divine realms, with source, with archangels, and indeed with your higher self bringing all of this light, making all of this Divine love accessible to all within the physical realm, for all of humanity at this time on planet earth.

And so indeed, we are connected now to increase the clarity of your experience. I invite you to take a deep breath, in through your nose filling your entire being with the white light flowing your way now.

Breathe and relax.

Quiet your mind by focusing on a blank screen before you. In this way you are able to quiet your ego mind, and the voice of doubt, and judgment, while leaving the screen of your mind's eye open for impressions from the Divine and angelic realms to come through.

Understand, we proceed at the pace that is right for you, and so you may think that you desire a profound, an eye opening psychic experience of connecting with your angels, but until you put in the work of releasing filters and increasing your vibration, these filters of mind, of the physical realm will block much of the etheric and spiritual experience from your knowing.

We will address this now, removing another layer of filtration blocking you from your direct experience with the Divine. As read these words, breathe, and open your heart, as we are joined by many angels of the light, many guides of light and, indeed ascended masters and archangels who simultaneously broadcast an uplifting frequency of unconditional love your way.

These blessings, vibrations, and healing emanations of Divine love are sent on strands of light. You may imagine that from where you are sitting, suddenly little pins of light, streams of light, strands of light, pour into this space and time, entering in through the space in between realms, entering into your physical location and proximity from the space between, the void, the pause between words, the silence found within the inner realms, and the absence of space. Light, love, and uplifting frequency flow your way.

Imagine that you are setting your mind on a shelf to simply look at this blank screen of light before you. Not to judge or analyze the experience, but to simply observe and be aware, for it is within this mode of perceiving reality through awareness, and through consciousness, that you are able to increase the scope of what you are perceiving and experiencing.

Understand that with your human being filters, you are largely focused in the physical realm. And yet you exist across multiple dimensions and times and places.

You exist in the physical, in the etheric, in the astral, and in high light, fine vibrations as your spiritual, higher self which is in close proximity, and direct communion with source, and with the Divine at all times. The blessing in this, is that you are able to practice, you are able to release the filters which block you from experiencing the magnificence of Divine love. And when you do this, you are able to lift and unite with the full truth of who you are, which indeed encompasses your ability to connect directly with the Divine; to see, hear, sense, and know in the angelic realms, and to know and understand the desires, the guidance, and the wisdom of your higher self.

Your higher, spiritual self knows your soul objectives for this life, and knows and understands that your possessions, things, and material objects may seem important and valuable to your personality self at this time, but to your higher self, to your soul and spirit, it is only the spiritual, emotional, and personal growth (the learning, seeking, and advancement that you are able to experience in this time) that stays with your soul as you journey forward. Growth through the spiritual planes stays with your soul over the course of many lifetimes and experiences. And so the ascension of your personal vibration as you lift and unite, and learn to pave the path to connect with the higher realms will come easier to you in lifetimes to come, and with enough growth, with enough increase in frequency and love in this life, you are able to leap forward in your conscious evolution and progression.

You are able to take a quantum leap forward on your journey of spiritual growth in this lifetime now. As a soul, this is of the utmost importance, for in every life your soul learns and grows and advances. What we are saying to you now, is the growth potential to be experienced in this life, contains more possibility, more significant opportunity for advancement than any life you have lived in the past thousand years. Right now, right here, a huge opportunity is available and all you must do to capitalize upon this prime moment in time and space is to commit, to make lifting in vibration a priority, to be willing to explore the inner spiritual realms.

When you put in the time and focus to fully activate your chakras of your physical and spiritual bodies, to lift in light and love, you are able to fully experience the angelic realms and the blessings held for you therein.

Right now an orb of light is placed around you, created out of the strands of light broadcast by many beings of Divine love, compassion, and healing. Imagine that in this orb of light your conscious awareness now begins to lift and this orb of light is passing through a sort of screen, a light screen, a light table, a platform of light that you begin to lift up and through. Up out the top of your crown chakra, up out the top of your head, up above the physical realm, up above space, up above time, up above the realm of illusion, up above this platform of light, and as you pass through this light table, screen, filter, your filter blocking you from experiencing the angelic and Divine realms are released. Know that this can only happen one layer at a time. And so to expose the full magnificence of your higher self, to fully connect with your gifts and your ability to clearly see Divine love and in the angelic realms, your filters must be peeled back like flower petals opening, like layers of an onion pulled back and away. Layers of doubt, of judgment, of limiting belief, thought forms and patterns, ideas which do not serve, filters centering you in the physical realm, blocking you from experiencing the Divine realms of peace and light must be exposed and released.

Humanity as a whole, Earth as one collective consciousness unit still has far to go towards becoming fully aligned with the Divine. The blessing is that you, beloved one, are able to ease the burden of this transition, for your personal growth and willingness and increased frequency ends not with you. As you increase your light, as you let down the filters, and as you unite with more of your brilliant light and radiance, this light ripples throughout the collective fields of consciousness, the one unit of all that is. Your increased light brings the blessings of well being and Divine love to all in your realm. Taking down these filters, and peeling back the onion, serves in many ways, serves all, but serves you in re-remembering.

Before you were born you existed in direct proximity with God, with light, with all angels and archangels and ascended masters. These realms are still available to you now.

Filters are still in place even when you are in spirit, but know that the filters you release now, the filters you remove from your expression in this life will not return.

To fully advance as a spiritual being, life is required. To fully release the filters and to experience Divine love and blessing; practice, persistence, focus, and life experience are your allies.

Having released a layer of your filters now, I Archangel Michael, now invite your guardian angel to once again make their presence known to you. To enter in and connect directly with you now. Know that this connection with your guardian angel occurs through your heart, throat chakra, third eye, and crown. As all of these upper energy centers receive a Divine alignment now, let yourself relax and open to begin tuning into the presence of your guardian angel, who has entered into this Divine space, this moment of time above the platform of light where a level of filtration has been released and where you are able to experience their love and blessing and frequency.

Your guardian angel now begins to broadcast more frequency, blessing, and healing which is custom designed to help you with whatever struggles or issues you are battling right now. Your guardian angel energetically assists you with whatever life lesson, or challenge, or opportunity is presented before you.

A new orb of light forms around you, healing, uplifting, and soothing your mental, emotional, and spiritual being.

Breathe and relax and I, Archangel Michael, now ask on your behalf;

"Beloved guardian angel, what is this beloved one's next step in increasing clarity of connection with the angelic realm?"

Quiet your mind, open your heart, and feel.

Receive an impression, see or hear this answer.

"What is your next step in moving forward and fully uniting with the angelic realm?"

Whatever you receive, let it be okay. It may make more sense in the days to come, or you may have only received a frequency download and blessing to help you with this objective.

Divine love is ever present, and as you tune into love, your vibration lifts. With a higher vibration, you are able to access the angelic realms. You lift in frequency and we lower in vibration. We meet you in a spiritual realm, in an etheric realm, and much of the communication is telepathic. Much of what you will see happens clairvoyantly. What you hear, occurs not audibly but psychically. And so developing these, your psychic senses, is of the utmost importance in fully experiencing the angelic realm.

As you have learned, and I reiterate now, fully opening your chakras to the highest possible degree enables these energy centers to filter the pure, white light of the Divine and translate it in a way that you are able to understand. Your chakras are a form of spiritual filtration. Not blocking out your spiritual experience, like filters of mind or density, but translating complex, singular, white light into wisdom, healing, guidance, and love, into tangible forms of thought and expression which are able to benefit you and all.

Imagine the orb of light which lifted you up into the realm of your guardian angel, now beginning to lower down around your being. You stay in this high vibrational place. This orb is like a spotlight scanning your body, looking for any places where stagnant energy resides, where density, energy of others, or soul blockages are preventing you from proceeding further. This white light scans your being and as it does, notice if anywhere in your body tenses up. As this happens, the light flows to those tense areas with increased frequency, dissipating blockages, releasing soul blockages into the light according to the Divine will to assist you now in progressing forward towards directly experiencing the full Divinity and light available to you at this time.

Breathe and relax as this orb of light continues to scan your body, releasing stuck energy which serve as another sort of filter blocking you from the full magnificent experience of the higher spiritual realms, that are possible for you to commune with in this life. Again, putting in the work and focus and time to make the link with your higher self, and with the archangelic realm, and indeed, with your guardian angel, brings blessings into many aspects of reality. But perhaps the most exciting from our perspective, is the removing of filters, which is permanent, and which stays with your soul forever. Removing filters that block you from experiencing Divine love from your current vantage point. Let these go. Let go of blocks go, let go of dense, stagnant energy, let go of pain and any state of dis-ease.

Accept this cleanse from the Divine now, and recognize that, indeed you have received a cleanse. You are now able to lift higher. And so hand in hand, heart to heart, we lift together now up above the lights, up above the universe, up above the astral realms, up above the realm of angels, and into direct presence with God, with Source, with the one energy making up All That Is. This is, direct experience with the highest frequency available to you now. From this place, by making this link, you are able to enter into the realm of archangels, you are able to merge with the full light of your higher self, with the ascended masters, and with all realms and dimensions of beings safely, without many potential of the detriments that come from directly entering into those realms from the physical.

Unite first with All, with Source, with God, with the one energy making up All That Is, and feel your oneness with this. This is the mode that archangels largely reside in, fully experiencing the complex Divinity of the one source energy and then manifesting into form as needed, when called upon, and to accomplish simple or specific objectives.

In this same way, you are able to merge with All That Is, to commune with all the blessings of the universe by connecting directly with source. And from this place, specific invitation of an archangel, nature angel, or spirit guide of the light, or even your higher self can be called in.

"At this time, we now invite your life angel of the light, or spirit guide of the light for this life, who is most aligned in helping you to accomplish your objectives. Come in, and connect at this time."

Be aware, and feel your energy merge with this, your life guide or angel. They may come in over the top of your head. Remember, it is your upper chakras that allow you to translate their pure, Divine frequency into words, images, feelings, and ideas.

Open your heart to feel the love. Open your mind's eye, your throat chakra, enabling clear communication, your crown to experience the wisdom that this, your life guide, offers you now.

Encouragement, blessings, and love, this is where your angels will always begin. We have the utmost respect for you and the journey you are upon. Angelic aid is always available in increasing frequency and strength as you lift, connect, and unite with the realms of spirit.

Before we leave, a simple process you can repeat again and again to connect with All.

To prepare yourself to invite in your angels and guides and higher self, simply breathe and relax.

Feel your energy ground. Connect to Earth, connect to Source, connect to All. Feel your oneness with All, with the light at the core of the Earth, and now that imagine this light from the core of the Earth begins to flow up. Let it clear, open, and activate all 7 chakras of your physical body. Continue to lift up with this light as your upper chakras, 8, 9, 10, 11, and 12, are cleared, activated, and opened.

Continue to lift up even more, into the light, above the light, above the platform of light, above the universe, above the angelic realm, above the ascended masters, above your higher self, into direct presence with Source, with Light, with God, with All That Is.

From this space, feel your oneness, feel your connection, know that All That Is, is connected with you. I, Archangel Michael, am your other God self. You are my other God self. All That Is, is made up of God, of one light. Feel this love and from this place we now invite the full presence of your higher self to enter in to unite with you in this time and place, to uplift you spiritually, mentally, emotionally, and to bring healing to you physically. Feel this merge.

Your higher self may have a message for you right away, or the feeling may be the more important message to convey at this time. Do not judge, but be open to whatever you experience now as you unite with your higher self. In this same way, from direct connection with God and Source, you are able to invoke an archangel, nature angel, your guardian angel, or a spirit guide.

In presence of light, of God, and of All That Is, think or say:

"I now invite Archangel Michael to connect with me now."

Whoosh.

Feel the increase of frequency after these words have been spoken. Feel my presence unite with you in this now. Lift in the love, bask in the Divine presence. Heal in this uplifting frequency, and when you are ready, ground the light of your higher self, of the Divine, of the archangels, of your guardian angel into your body, grounding into physical from.

This is not to say release the high vibrational energies you are connecting with and embracing. It simply means to bring them into your physical life, to ground them to the Earth, to bring the light of the archangels and the Divine into present time, to make this high vibrational frequency your normal mode of being. To vibrate with love and peace and joy as your default, as your normal state of being. You will need to practice in order for this to fully stick.

Lift, connect with the magnificence of the Divine and the angels. Commune directly with these high vibrational beings of light and love. Directly connect with the Divine, and then carry this uplifted vibration with you throughout your daily life. Share this light freely with all. Remove the filters blocking you from directly experiencing the etheric and spiritual realms.

Increase your vibration, open your chakras, and then through your meditation, magnificent experience of connecting with the angelic realm is made possible for you.

We cannot do all the work for you, for you are a conscious being with free will. But as you uplift in frequency, we will respond, and meet you in the middle. As you put in the work, we will assist you in progressing further. As you remove the filters and density and negativity which block you from directly experiencing the Divine realms of love; you will learn to see, hear, sense, know, feel, and understand clearly in the realm of angels. This is not impossible for you, this is made possible through the light of the Divine, claim this connection, it is your birthright.

Claim this ability to connect. Increase your vibration and let go of the filters which keep you focused only in the physical realm and know that, yes, you are able to be present in physical and to be aware in the realms of spirit simultaneously. This is a gift which we offer to you, and as you practice lifting and connecting, directly experiencing source, and then focusing this light energy through your chakras you will experience your guardian angel, you will experience the archangels, and experience your angels and spirit guides of the light, and your higher self. When you do this, you are serving your life, and you are bringing joy and excitement and learning into the present time. This benefits all of humanity, but even more, the growth you experience heals along the lines of time bringing forgiveness and healing to your ancestors: past, present, and future. And the gifts of spirit, the cornucopia of blessings which you are able to tune into through connecting with the angelic realm stays with your soul forever.

There is great benefit in making the link, in putting in the work, in practicing, and in seeking the Divine love of angels. Practice will make perfection. This is possible for you now. Lift, open, intend, connect.

I am Archangel Michael and I will always answer when called upon. Increase your vibration and frequency first to clearly hear, understand, and benefit from the angelic teachings which are always available for you.

We angels leave you now with a final blessing and initiation into the realms of angelic love. Strands of light enter into this present place and time to cleanse and uplift you.

Finally now, an orb of light forms above your crown. A waterfall of light gently pouring down, cleansing your chakras of any negative residue, of any filtration system which no longer serves. Any lingering soul blockages, density, and patterns of struggle are released. By this waterfall of light, according to Divine will, you are now cleansed, uplifted, blessed, and greatly loved.

Use what you have learned, practice an increase in light, connect with the archangelic, angelic, and spiritual realms often, for many blessings are available therein. We are so pleased to watch you progress, to open, to release your filters, and to shine the full magnificent light of your higher self that you are. Bring this full light into physical form.

You are supported and you are loved. I am Archangel Michael. I now leave you with love and with my blessing. Goodbye for now.

7

Connecting With Your
Higher Self

~ Orion

Dear One. Indeed I Orion am pleased to connect with you in this very time and space, this moment of moments during which much more is going on that meets the eye. You see in this one moment, you are connected to an infinite number of moments, of possibilities of alternate realities or dimensions some may say, all interconnected. Past, present, future, parallel alternate realities and scenarios are all interwoven and meeting in the present moment, in this now.

In this now, there is an unlimited amount of support, guidance and wisdom available for you beyond the veil, in this moment, in this very moment there is healing frequency, love, and compassion which you can tune into to re-calibrate your path. To re-align with the Divine plan and blueprint for your life, which was laid out with your assistance, while you were still in spirit. But understand, that you still have presence in the spiritual realm. These spiritual aspects of you exist in a vibration closely resembling that of your angels and guides, in a dimension of the inner realms.

Your soul, your spiritual self, or your higher self, is directly connected to Divine Source and to all wisdom, knowledge, truth, understanding and love. The benefit for you in re-uniting with your full spiritual self and light, and anchoring this wisdom, power, frequency and love into your physical being is that then all this is accessible by you. All the gifts of the Divine, the cornucopia of blessings, abundance and love available for you.

For when you are connected with the authentic truth of who you are, when you are brightly shining with an illumi-nated mind, vibrant body, and awakened spirit; your psychic gifts of clairvoyance, intuition, spiritual vision, telepathy with your guides and angels, understanding and awareness of the greater multiverse around you is made known. The knowing of your authentic path, of your next steps, of your true heart and souls desires are known to you, and with this awareness, and with your power and your light intact, you are able to progress forward. You are able to ex-perience profound and lasting growth from where you are right now. And so I Orion am pleased to assist you now in connecting with that which is your higher self, your spiri-tual self, or your authentic soul self. The process for con-necting is fairly simple. I will walk you through it entirely.

To begin, let yourself relax. Let your mind be still. Read these words and notice now that as the words continue to flow across the page before you, your mood, your vibra-tion, and your frequency is being uplifted.

Focus within as you read. Open your heart and consciously enter in.

Open your heart and simultaneously, I Orion and your guides and angels lift you up in awareness, and in consciousness to become aware of the realms beyond the physical. In awareness you are now lifted up above the physical realm up, and above the very universe which you are apart of. Up and above the lights, above the angelic realm, above the higher dimensions where ascended masters and ancestors dwell, up above the lights, and into direct presence with Source. With Divine love. With All That Is. With God. Breathe, and notice how good it feels to be in this space and presence. Notice the presence of healing frequency being broadcast to your body, to your mind and yes to your spirit in this place of conscious connection.

Breathe. Relax. Let this Divine love flow all around you, illuminating your being, and increasing your level of awareness, and now in this space of Source, of God of Light, on your behalf, we now invite the full presence and might, the full love and light ,of your higher self to enter in. The light of your spiritual and authentic self lowers down, uniting with you in this very now, through the realm of the heart, the portal of the heart, the sacred passageway within to the realms of Divine love, to spirit, to the angelic realms, and to the light.

Now, as your vibration continues to lift with the assistance of your guides and angels on the inner planes, your soul light and the full vibration of your higher self lowers down. You meet in the middle.

Your spirit, your body, and mind are uniting now through the realm of your heart, and through the conscious awareness of love. Uniting now, lifting you, and merging with your higher self.

Focus upon your heart. Relax and breathe. Let the energy flow, let your self merge with your full soul light. Allow the full qualities of your higher self, your spirit, download now into your physical being, and into your physical life.

Allow the gifts of spirit, the gifts of your light, the unique and authentic strengths, attributes and skills, which your soul has carried from lifetime to lifetime return to you now. Skills which you have learned and built upon over lifetimes, utilized to evolve to, grow and to advance within. Remember the in-life lessons you have mastered, and carried with you forward on the path of the awakening and awareness, even after death.

The full extent of your soul growth is expansive. Let all the knowing, and the wisdom, the skills, the talents, the love, of your soul, of your higher self and spirit, download now into the present moment where you can access it all. Download now into the realm of the heart.

Open your heart to this your soul light, and let these Divine qualities of love, of compassion, of ability and of increased frequency download now. Divine love. Divine mind. Divine body. Divine spirit. Divine will, hope, compassion, download now.

This energy flows through in through the top of your head, through the crown chakra. Relax to let it flow all the way down your spinal column, activating and opening all your chakras. Cleansing you with the light of the Divine and continuing to flow down now through the bottom of your feet. And as you breathe out, now ground this your spiritual light, your gifts, your talents, your soul strengths.

Ground the light of your higher self and soul into your heart, and into the Earth, into the physical realm, into the intricate web of energy which you are a part of, which you are one with, and by infusing your soul qualities into this one life force energy, transformation begins, and will continue through your increased awareness for dear one the link has been made. The link with your higher self, your soul, your spirit has been made in this now.

With the assistance from your guides and angels from I Orion, from Jesus, from Mother Mary, we are all here and have witnessed this link of your physical being with your full spiritual light. You are beautiful and radiant in this life.

When your heart is open you are able to re-link, to strengthen the link with your higher self is to honor the light of your soul in every moment. And so to merge with your higher self from this point forward, it is simple. Feel your energy ground, to connect with the Earth and with all that is. Open your heart, quiet your mind, enter in, and then lift on one thousand wings of love. Your angels are always accessible, when you enter into your heart, you open a portal a direct passageway to the Divine.

Think. Seek. Go up. Seek God. Seek Source. Seek the Divine. Lift into the light, from within a place of awareness found within your open heart.

Then think or say, "I now invite the full light of my higher self, of my soul, of my light body, of my full spiritual awareness, to downward now. Connect with me now. Merge with me now."

Open your heart, and listen, this is all you must do. The merge is made. The light is accessible. Your soul light is present.

Bask in the beauty of this Divine love. Find the silence in this space, the healing in this space, feel the love present through this connection, and simply be.

You are connected now to your higher self. Practice listening for this voice of wisdom that is connected to infinite intelligence, and to All That Is.

All knowing, all understanding, all wisdom, is found within you. Your ego mind and your personality may think it knows more. But the truth is, your higher self and your soul, is connected is to all wisdom, truth, and understanding.

And so quiet your mind, open your heart, and listen through the sacred portal of your heart. Dismiss thought as it comes into your awareness. Return to the stillness, qualities of love within your heart, and at this time on your behalf we ask your higher self, your soul, to broadcast clearly and distinctly a message for you now.

Whatever it is you most need to know now, quiet your mind, open your heart, and receive. Through the stillness, and through this connection through your heart, the wisdom of your soul and higher self is accessible.

You may ask a question, you may focus your meditation with intention, but then listen and be aware. Feel, witness, and experience, for the knowledge will be conveyed in multiple forms. Perhaps you will clearly hear the answer, or feel, or simply know. You may receive a vision, a smell, or you may even receive a loving thought. Be open and be aware. Practice.

Link daily with the light of your soul as this benefits you, and broadcasts a ripple of love and positivity through the energy signature which you are always sending. When you are united with your full spirit, and infused with Divine love, you have made the link, link often, and then return. Ground your full spiritual light into the physical. Utilize your gifts your abilities, your love Listen and tune into the awareness and knowing of your soul, and then take action. This leads to harmony, balance, fulfillment, increased love and qualities of the Divine, which you deserve.

As we now part, we first download you once more with Divine love, Divine will, Divine compassion Divine trust, Divine joy and with the full light of your Divine spirit and higher self, download now.

Now as I, Orion begin to pull away, I increase the light frequency which flows your way. As we break our energetic connection feel your energy ground. Claim all this light you have connected with, all of these Divine qualities of your higher self and of the angelic realm. Claim the love, grounding it into the physical, into the Earth. Feel roots flowing down, light flowing down, where you then are able to connect to the Earth. Experience your oneness with Earth, with All, with love, you are one.

You are light. You are love, and these qualities of the Divine will serve you in ushering positive change into your experience and into the greater collective consciousness of humanity. Love serves you. You are love. Unite with the full Divine light of your spirit, and allow the blessings from this connection to emerge. I now leave you with this surge of light and frequency, and with love, and blessings.

Ground this all. Claim this. You are so loved. Goodbye for now.

8

High Vibrational Atunement

~ Archangel Metatron

Greetings beloved one. Indeed I am Archangel Metatron present here and now broadcasting light. Broadcasting an infinite supply of divine frequency from the higher realms, into your present space and time, and into this very moment.

I am here to assist you in letting go of your ego mind for just a moment. Letting go of rational thought, worry, and stress. Let go, and enter inward.

Imagine before your minds eye a blank slate, and focus within.

Visualize the doors of your heart opening wide as you consciously drop in, entering into your inner sacred space found within your open heart. Here you are able to access the infinite guidance of your heart and of your soul.

Building upon this, as you lift in vibration, you are able to access the guidance of your angels, spiritual beings of love, the ascended masters and saints, who guide you from the other side.

Spiritual beings who guide, support, and love you unconditionally from the realms of spirit. Who ever so subtlety, align blessings and synchronicity on your path when you ask for help, and when you ask for guidance.

When you think upon these beings, these spiritual masters, and invite their essence, presence, and love into your life, the synchronicity, alignments, guidance, and divine placements upon your path can be increased tenfold. Allow the miraculous, the extraordinary, and the beautiful to be experienced by you in every moment, for these energies are always present all around you, waiting for you to tune in.

This is the power of gratitude. Noticing and appreciating what is beautiful around you, attracts more beauty, magnificence, and miracles into your experience.

This is the benefit in lifting your vibration, which we will assist with in shortly. Lifting your vibration is made possible in every moment through your thought, through your action, and through your point of perspective.

When you change the way you perceive what is happening around you, what is happening around you changes, indeed. Viewing your reality through the lens of love allows love to be mirrored unto you in a vast array of possibility and potential.

Love focused upon builds and grows. Love is truly available for you in an infinite supply from the divine, from the angelic realms, from the ascended masters, from saints, from your spirit guides, and all you must do is breathe, quiet your thoughts, and tune in.

Do not worry if your mind interrupts, and bombards you with thought. Let yourself focus upon the thought for a moment. Acknowledge the thought which appears.

Think or say to the thought, "I see you, you are mine, I acknowledge you," for with this perspective, not judging yourself for having a thought but rather simply acknowledging the thought, you're then able to let it go.

Return to silence, stillness, and calm. Focus within, breathe, and let go.

Feel your energy, and all aspects of yourself, all of your frequency and your personal power gathering in this very moment, gathering in your heart center area.

Now feel your energy ground. Imagine your energy flowing down, connecting you to the earth, connecting you to earth and to all that is. From this grounded, centered, calm, relaxed, and aware perspective you are now ready, able, and if you are willing to, lift.

Imagine you are beginning to float up. Simultaneously, your guides and angels broadcast frequency supporting you in your journey upward, supporting you in journeying into the divine realms. Lift into the realms of spirit, lift in happiness and in love, on the wings of your angels.

Go up, lift up, float up into the divine realms in consciousness and in frequency. Imagine, it is happening, imagine it is so. Perceive the spiritual realms now, not with your physical senses, but rather with your imagination.

Subtlety feeling, knowing, experiencing the white light, the divine light that is, indeed, all around you. Lift and breathe in white light of the Divine, which soothes your being, calms your nerves, and eases any tension or anxiety.

White light which elevates your vibration and paves the pathway for you to reconnect time and time again with the divine realms, where you are present here and now. The divine realms where you are able to call upon your guides, your guardian angels, the saints and ascended masters who can most serve you in claiming the blessings available for you in every moment. Blessings are present indeed, and when focused upon, they build and grow.

Simply think or say now, "Guides, angels, ascended masters... What insight, healing, or wisdom do you have for me now?"

Imagine you're opening your heart wider, imagine you are opening your energy up to receive this blessing of frequency, guidance and love.

Let it in, breathe it in, embrace it, know it, understand it, this communion you are experiencing now with spiritual beings who love you unconditionally. Spiritual beings who desire for nothing more than to assist you in living your authentic truth, which is joyful, radiant, well, inspired, and fulfilled. We hold this vision for you.

Through your connection with the Divine, which you have made, your purpose is magnified before you. When you move in the direction of joy, of excitement, and passion, you are on track.

When you express gratitude for the little aspects, the tiny things you love in your reality, they are able to grow and build.

Love in every moment is the master path before you, which allows new blessings into your life. Blessings which know no limit.

There is an infinite supply of love, of the vibration that is miraculous, available through your communion, connection, and oneness with the Divine, with the angels, with the ascended masters, and with all that is.

At this time we invite the saint or ascended master, who can most serve you now, to please step forward.

This may be a being you are familiar with, whom you have learned about, or maybe someone new. Be willing to accept the quality, the frequency, that this beloved guide offers you now.

Become aware of their message for you. Become aware of the meaning this connection holds for you right now be it healing, encouragement, attunement, introduction, forgiveness or simply love.

Receive the blessing from the saint or ascended master. This spiritual being who has walked upon the earth, who has seen reality through the perspective you view it now and who has mastered their lessons of life.

This saint or ascended master is stepping forward now to help you to master your lessons, your soul objectives, your purpose for being here in the classroom of life.

Mastery over your emotions, mastery in terms of mental control, mastery in terms of your physical vitality, and mastery in terms of your spiritual connection. Mastery of life does not only mean making a lot of money, or even being a spiritual person.

Mastery of life includes every aspect of life, harmoniously interwoven together in a way which is fulfilling for you, empowering for you, and for others. Seeing the blessings all around you, within you, and in others, seeing the light in others, seeing the Divine in others. This is the enlightened perspective you are able to shift into when you let go of fear and doubt.

Know that this perspective benefits you, and the ripple of positivity created from this serves all, for you are connected with all of humanity, with all beings, with all that is. Your growth and commitment to increasing your vibration, expanding your joy, living love, living in a state of fulfillment and alignment with your soul desire allows this to be made possible for others as well.

A small pebble dropped into the pool of infinite possibility creates a ripple of magnificent effect throughout the vast field of oneness that encompasses all that is.

You are a part of all, you are one with all, and so it is.

At this time feel and be aware of your expanded sense of self. Feel your connection to everyone and to everything as your awareness returns to your individual aura, energy, and physical body.

The energy of all that is, now cleansed and purified, is contained within your cells, within your whole, within your mind, body, spirit.

The energy of all that is, the vast network of connections...

Life, love, gratitude and well being aligned in your being, compressed into a compact, high vibrational light being, spiritual being, alive, vibrant, present in physical form. You.

You are so loved, blessed, and lifted. Carry this light with you throughout your life, for doing so makes a tremendous difference. Choose love. Draw love to you and witness the connections occurring as love builds upon love and expands outward throughout all that is.

I am Archangel Metatron. On behalf of the many guides, angels, ascended masters, and saints present with you now, we bow to the Divine in you. We bow to the divine light that you are, to the magnificence, brilliance, and love that you are.

Live this truth divine spiritual being. Express your light and live as the authentic, empowered, radiant spiritual being that you are.

We leave you now with our love and blessing. Goodbye for now.

Bonus .MP3 Meditation

Connect with Your Guides and Angels
~ Angelic Guide Orion

"You have a life guide, your spirit guide who is with you for your entire life, and indeed, you have additional guides and angels who come in to help you here in the physical."

~ Orion

Access this bonus .MP3 Meditation with the Angelic Guide Orion here: **www.ask-angels.com/experiencing-angels-bonus-meditations**

Experience Angels
Audio Meditation Series

Access the 7 Angel Messages, which make up Experience Angels, as Original .MP3 Audio Meditations, set to the beautiful meditative music of Thaddeus.

Visit The Following Link For More Information, or to Purchase; **www.ask-angels.com/angel-courses/angel-course-experienceangels**

About The Author

Melanie Beckler is a clear Angelic Channel of the Light. She feels both honored and blessed to share the ever unfolding and expanding guidance, love, and upliftment that flows through as a result of her direct connection with the Realm of Angels.

Melanie continues to focus on publishing high energy meditations, angel courses, and Kindle Books of Angel Messages, to assist those awakening to their spiritual light, paths, and purpose.

For more information regarding Melanie's work, visit her website

www.Ask-Angels.com

Youtube Channel

youtube.com/askangels

Twitter

twitter.com/askangels

Or Facebook Page

facebook.com/AskAngelsFan

Excerpt from
Let Your Light Shine

Cleanse and Connect With Your Angels
~Archangel Michael

Beloved one, indeed, I am Archangel Michael and I am here with you now, with you always. I invite you to now connect with me deeply, profoundly for your benefit and for the benefit of manifesting that which you desire into the physical. For, understand, when your heart is open, when you are connected to your angels and attuned to love you are able to flow with the natural course of reality. You are able to manifest blessings of love, joy, health, and abundance in your life.

To connect with the angelic realm, all you must do is relax, breathe, and open your heart. The angelic realm exists very near to your own physical realm. In many senses we angels are only a breath away. And so as you take in a deep breath of fresh, healing air now, allow your conscious awareness to drop into your heart. Open your heart chakra now. Open your heart and open the doors to the angelic realm therein to instantly feel, sense, hear, smell, know, feel the love of your angels that are indeed all around.

Think or say, "Angels surround me. angels lift my vibration. angels guide me, help me upon my path." Know that when you ask, we answer. Every time you ask for angelic assistance we are always happy to assist. Know that the more you practice, the more you open, the more you lift your own vibration by choosing and living love; the more clearly, the more accurately, and the more profoundly our guidance, love, and presence will appear in your life. Part of this process, indeed, is raising your vibration. You are able to do this by releasing the lower vibrations of density, fear, and negativity that still dwell within your being. Releasing and replacing these lower vibrations with love, with compassion, with joy, and with light. As you consciously practice this, you lift, you become more compassionate, more closely connected to the full light of your soul... You ascend. Your vibration becomes more closely attuned to the realm of angels and you are able to experience our love, our guidance, our light in your own life in the forms of living joyously, living in love, living inspired, living in alignment with your true and authentic purpose.

Now to cleanse your energy, to lift you into the realm of angels and light and love so that you may continue to increase your connection...

Relax, breathe, and imagine now that there is an orb of light above your head, angelic light, light of the Divine. This golden orb of light now begins to pour light down like a waterfall of light. When you're ready, step directly into this flow, let the light we angels broadcast, let this energy of Divine love flow all around you, cleansing those residues of fear, doubt, and negativity away. Clearing you mind, body, spirit.

Let go. Like holding a helium balloon out in front of you and loosening your grip. Let go of all that no longer serves you. Release past residue from your physical body, your emotional body, your etheric body, your light body.

Imagine this waterfall of light from above continues to pour down on you and when you are ready, open up your crown chakra at the top of your head by simple thinking it so and letting more light into your being. You may feel a tingling, a pulsing sensation as this light comes in. This light is connecting you with the angelic realm of love, with your unique spiritual gifts and psychic abilities; abilities to heal, to manifest, to live your inspired life, your Divine blueprint, your love in the physical.

Let your vibration continue to lift as this light pours in and all around you. And now at this time, with your permission, with your simply thinking, "Yes." I, Michael, agree to cut any and all cords that are draining you energetically, consciously or unconsciously. These draining cords, with your permission, are now cut and released into the light All energy that is yours that has been drained now returns to you cleansed, purified, and activated with love. All that remains in you that does not serve, that is not rightfully yours, that is not love is lifted up and out of your being now, beyond this orb of light above you, and into the light. And now you are cleansed and your vibration lifted. All you are left to do is quiet your mind, open your heart, feel the love of angels, and feel us wrap you with our wings of love.

Lift, breathe, and now beloved, if you have a question, let yourself formulate this in your mind and then pay attention to the thought, to the feeling, to the sense that your angels respond with.

Or if you would simply like to sit and bask in this energy of angelic love that is indeed all around you. We will stay with you and continue to nurture, to love, and to lift your vibration.

The more often you connect with this energy of your open heart, consciously reflecting, and opening your senses beyond the physical, the more you are able to pick up the love, the guidance, and the messages of your angels. Feel this love now, radiate this love, and share this love with others.

You are blessed and you are lifted, you are cleansed. Now shine your light and continue forward on your path, if you will, to feel, to know, to fully experience the light of your angels and the light of your inner Divine being and higher self. All accessible in every moment simply a breath away. Open your heart and tune in to the angelic realm therein. *I am Archangel Michael, and you are so dearly loved.*

Acknowledgements

Firstly, thank you, for reading and for reaching upwards to experience the Angelic Realm. Your personal growth and increased light makes a huge difference for us all.

Thank you to Rebecca, for your work transcribing the recorded channeled messages from the Angels which were used for this book. Thank you JB for your help with formatting, graphics, and for making the book function. Thank you Danilo for creating the beautiful Angel artwork which was modified for the cover, and to Paris for excellent proofreading.

Finally, thank you to my twin flame Miles, for sharing this life and adventure in connecting with all that is possible beyond the physical, and for believing in me, and loving me through it all.

Available Now
by Melanie Beckler

Open your heart and mind to experience the unconditional love and guidance of the Angelic Realm. Simply reading these messages from the angels will assist you in bringing more joy, healing, and spiritual fulfillment into your life. With the guidance and uplifting angelic frequency woven throughout these pages, you will be inspired, to Let Your Light Shine!

www.amazon.com/dp/B00AA59U9W

Manifesting blessings in your life and the lives of others is an important aspect of your true purpose here on Earth. As you build up your spiritual light, you are able to more easily share positive blessings and you become more protected from the negativity of every-day life. By reading these angel messages and tuning into the angelic frequencies they contain, you are able to connect with healing and bring more joy, love and abundance in to your life.

www.amazon.com/dp/B00BB8XLCE

Made in the USA
Lexington, KY
01 May 2017